Discovering

DISCOVERING SPIRITS:
Series Editor Charles MacLean

Discovering

Gin

GERALDINE COATES

DISCOVERING GIN

Geraldine Coates

First published in the United Kingdom in 1996 by
NewLifeStyle Publishing Limited, Christchurch,
Dorset and London

A CIP catalogue record for this book is available from the
British Library

ISBN 1 86095 007 8

Design by Crispin Goodall Design Ltd

Printed and bound in the United Kingdom by
Warwick Printing Co Ltd

CONTENTS

FOREWORD

I could not better Lord Kinross's marvellously apt
description of gin as the "ardent spirit which rose from
the gutter to become the respected companion of
civilised man".

In my telling of the story of gin, many people have helped
me. I would like to thank my children, my family, Robert
McDowell, Charles MacLean and my colleagues at
Marketing Advantage. I am grateful also to Nicholas
Morgan of United Distillers, Richard Paterson of Whyte &
Mackay, J. S. Hogg, Desmond Payne of Beefeater, Sarah
Jobson of Scope Communications, The Food Programme,
The Gin and Vodka Association, Ian Wright at The Central
Library, Edinburgh, Philip Woyka, my publishers and the
many gin and other companies who have given me help
and information and provided illustrations.

Read, enjoy.
Geraldine Coates
Edinburgh 1995

ACKNOWLEDGEMENTS

David Parfitt (Photograph page 78).
Sara Midda (Illustration page 79).
Bridgeman Art Library; pages 6, 20, 21, 23, 25, 26, 53.
Mary Evans Picture Library; pages 22, 28, 30, 21, 32, 35, 37,
38, 40, 44, 48, 59.
Ronald Grant Archive; pages 77, 79.

*The name for the end
product of the distiller's
craft is to be found in most
European languages as a
translation of 'the water
of life.'*
  *eau de vie in French
  aquae vitae in Italian
  akvavit in Swedish
  usquebaugh in Gaelic*

PART 1: WHAT IS GIN?

What is gin? The straightforward answer is that it is clear, rectified, unaged alcohol which has been further distilled together with a variety of fruit and herb flavourings, principally juniper.

Behind this bald statement of fact lies a fascinating story, a story which has its beginnings at the dawn of human history.

All the evidence points to distilling as one of the most ancient arts, known in every culture from the ancient Chinese onwards. Strangely there is no historical agreement on where and when it was first discovered and practised. Distilling was brought to Europe by the Arabs who practised it to make perfumes and rose-water.

Because there were no vines in Northern Europe great efforts were made to produce a potable spirit from the readily available grain crops and, from about the twelfth to

THE CONTINUOUS STILL
*The flow lines demonstrate
the path of the alcohol-
bearing wash on its way to
pure spirit.*

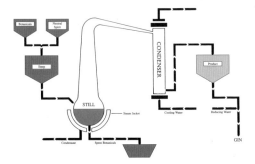

*Left: The Apothecary (also
known as the chemist).
Gabriel Metsu (1629-67)*

the fourteenth centuries, the distilling of alcohol was
constantly experimented with.

Distillation itself is a simple process. Alcohol comes to
the boil before water, so, when a fermented liquor is
heated, the alcohol in it will rise in the form of a vapour.
The vapour is then run off and cooled. As it cools, it
returns to a liquid form which is the spirit. Spirits can be
made from any raw material containing starch or sugar
which is first fermented and then distilled.

*European distilling had its
origins in the mediaeval
kitchen, particularly those of
the large monasteries which
experimented with herbs
and spices to manufacture
medicinal cordials and
liqueurs.*

PROOF OF ALCOHOL

The amount of alcohol in a bottle is usually expressed as a percentage of its contents today - x% 'Alcohol by Volume' (ABV). Formerly it was expressed as 'degrees proof'. This was measured by adding gunpowder to the spirit: if it did not ignite it was 'under proof' (i.e. under 100°); when it lit and burned steadily it was deemed to be 'of proved strength' or 'at proof' (i.e. 100°); if it exploded it was (over proof) (over 100°).

100° proof in the U.S.A.
= 87.7° British proof
= 50% ABV
100° proof in Britain
= 114.2° U.S.A. proof
= 57.1% ABV
40% ABV
= 70° proof (British)

The Pure Spirit

The pure spirit which is the base for today's gin is made through a process of continuous distillation in a Patent Still, invented in 1830 by Aeneas Coffey, a Dublin Excise Officer.

The modern version of the Coffey Still consists of two parallel columns each containing a series of perforated plates. The cold wash, i.e. the alcohol bearing liquid (in the case of premium gin usually a fermentation of maize), is fed at the top of the Rectifying column into a pipe which zigzags down the column where it is heated by steam passing up through the plates. It then crosses over into the next column, the Analyser. The warm liquid runs through the analyser and meets the steam rising upwards at the bottom of the column. The steam evaporates the more volatile elements of the wash including the alcohol while the rest, the spent wash, is drawn off at the bottom of the analyser. The vaporised alcohol passes into the bottom of the rectifier and, as it rises, it is warmed and in turn cooled as the new wash descends. The heavier elements of the wash condense and are removed from the bottom of the column. The good spirit turns back into liquid on its journey back up the rectifier. The most volatile elements reach the top of the column still as vapour and are drawn off to be re-distilled with the elements removed from the bottom of the pipe. These are known as feints or heads and tails and they are always separated from the heart of the distillation.

The pure neutral grain spirit which leaves the still at around 160° proof is the basis of gin. At this stage it is very similar to vodka and only acquires its distinctive taste when it is re-distilled with the botanical flavourings.

COLD COMPOUNDING

Reputable distillers will always re-distil the botanicals and the spirit together to produce the high quality gin of the premium brands. There is another method of making gin called 'cold compounding' where the botanicals, sometimes in the form of artificial flavourings, are added and mixed with the spirit which is generally a distillate of molasses. The result are greatly inferior gins which can be easily recognised by their perfumed, 'room freshener' smell and taste. Avoid them by always looking for the wording 'distilled gin' on the label when buying gin.

English law requires that the base alcohol is distilled in a different location from the second distillation. Distillers specify that the pure neutral spirit is made according to the special requirements of their brand and carry out extensive checks on each delivery against a sample to ensure quality and consistency. The final quality of the gin will depend very much on the purity of the spirit used.

The Distilling Process

All gin might appear the same to the casual drinker largely because flavours are often masked by the addition of mixers. In truth no two gins are alike and there are distinct variations in flavour between the leading brands of gin - of which more later. There are good gins and bad gins. Recipes are closely guarded secrets and some will date back two hundred years or more. A good gin is easily recognisable by its clean, natural flavour because reputable distillers will always use natural ingredients in their recipes.

All gin contains juniper which has given gin its name (from the French genievre) and was originally used for its medicinal value. Coriander

Knowledgeable distillers will tell you that, during the re-distilling process, the flavours of the botanicals come through at different times during the run. Orange peel is always the first.

seed is the other constant ingredient. Gin will also usually contain different proportions of lemon peel, orange peel, angelica, cassia bark and orris root. Some gins also include calamus root, liquorice and cinnamon.

The distinctively clean flavour of a premium gin can only be achieved by re-distillation. After the botanicals have been added to the neutral spirit the whole is traditionally re-distilled in a copper-pot still. During the process, the gin is constantly tested until it achieves a flavour which satisfies the ever vigilant head distiller. The gin is then reduced to the correct strength or proof by adding de-mineralised water and is filtered before bottling. In modern gin production, the overriding goal is to achieve quality which is consistent with the brand. This is a task which continues to demand skill, dedication and perseverance.

The design of the pot-still is crucially important as its shape will influence the rate at which the spirit vaporises. This in turn affects the flavour of the gin. At many distilleries original pot-stills are carefully preserved. At Gordon's for example there is one copper pot-still which has been in regular use for over 200 years.

As with the distilling of the pure spirit, the first and last parts of the run are discarded to be re-distilled as the flavour will not be consistent. The heart of the distillation is known as the 'middle cut'.

The best juniper berries come from Umbria and the leading distilleries go to great lengths to ensure that they are of the highest quality. First the berries are harvested in the traditional way by knocking the branches of each shrub with a stick. Distilleries will keep stocks of them maturing in hessian sacks. They take two years to ripen and are at their best just before they have reached maturity when they are rich in aromatic oil. The master distiller regularly samples the berries and decides which batches are ready for use.

The Botanicals

The Most Common Flavourings for Gin

Juniper

A small, prickly coniferous evergreen, the juniper grows throughout Europe. The berries turn a rich blue-black and take three years to ripen. Then the pungent, aromatic juniper oil which gives gin its distinctive flavour can be extracted. The best juniper berries are grown in Italy.

Coriander

Coriander originated on the eastern shores of the Mediterranean and has been cultivated for centuries throughout Asia. Coriander seeds have a fresh, mild, astringent flavour and have been used in herbal medicine for thousands of years. The oil has local anaesthetic properties and can ease muscular and rheumatic pain.

Angelica Root

Angelica originated in Iceland, Greenland and Northern Russia but is now naturalised throughout most of Europe, including the UK. Its sweetening properties are much valued in the kitchen and the root is used in traditional Chinese medicine.

Orange Peel

Sweet orange oil is mildly sedative and is often used as an anti-depressant. When combined with other oils, it can reduce insomnia.

Lemon Peel

Lemon oil is refreshing and invigorating with many ancient medicinal applications such as in the treatment of respiratory problems and sore throats, to fight infection, to aid skin tone and as a tonic to the circulation system.

Cassia bark

Cassia oil is extracted from cinnamon bark and tastes and smells very much like cinnamon but is stronger and more bitter. In China cassia is considered one of the great spices. It is often used in skin care and cassia extracts were mixed with almond oil to make Macassar oil - a popular Victorian hair oil for men.

Ginger

Ginger is an aromatic root originating from the jungles of South East Asia whose distinctive smell and fiery taste make it a popular ingredient in most types of cuisine. Ginger is much used in traditional Chinese medicine and has a reputation as an aphrodisiac.

Nutmeg

Nutmeg is widely used in Western and Eastern cooking, its warm sweet flavour with a slightly bitter undertone blending well with other spices. Its uses are extremely varied. For example it turns up as an essential ingredient of West Indian rum punch, Scottish haggis and traditional Christmas mince pies.

Orris Root Powder

This fragrant root is dried and ground down for talcum powder. The smell of sweet violets is associated with the

orris root and it is often used in pot-pourri mixes. Orris
grows in southern France and Italy and the 3-4 year old
plants are lifted in the autumn, dried and kept for two
years during which time their fragrance increases.

Liquorice Root
The liquorice plant is native to South-Eastern Europe and
the Middle East. Its roots descend below ground for about
I metre sending out horizontal rhizomes. It is these
rhizomes which are used as flavouring. The bitter sweet
liquorice root has been enjoyed as a natural confection for
thousands of years and is also widely used in the
treatment of coughs and bronchitis.

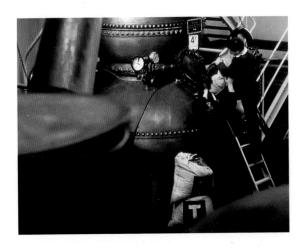

*Left: Stills being charged
with botanicals.*

A son of Henri IV invented a wine flavoured with juniper which had been drunk in France in the 15th century. It was known as 'the wine of the poor'.

PART II: THE GIN HERITAGE
The Birth of Gin

Appropriately for a drink which is much appreciated for its restorative powers, gin started life as medicine. Sylvius of Leyden, Professor of Medicine at the University of Leyden is generally credited with the perfection of a purified grain spirit flavoured with juniper, known as "eau de vie de genievre". In 1572, patients with intestinal disorders coming to Leyden for treatment were prescribed doses of this spirit. Its therapeutic value became widely known as its use spread from the Netherlands throughout Northern Europe.

Geneva seems to have made the leap from apothecary's shelf to tavern table effortlessly. Since the middle ages, the Dutch had made a crude form of spirit

THE FIRST RECIPE
The first recipe for making genevà - aqua juniperi was published in Amsterdam in 1622.

from cereals, mainly rye, known as 'brandewijn' *(burnt wine)*, the everyday term for all forms of spirit. This was rough tasting and constant experimentation was carried out to find a way of making it more palatable.

The juice of the juniper berry was found to be an effective flavouring agent and the commercial value of a

juniper flavoured distillate was quickly recognised. By 1572, Lucas Bols in Holland was commercially producing large quantities of *genever*, also known as *jenever*, or *Geneva*.

BOLS

It is believed that Lucas Bols was the first commercial distiller of genever. The genever industry grew up around the town of Schiedam near Rotterdam because the grain trade was situated there whilst liqueur making was concentrated on Amsterdam. In the 16th and 17th centuries Amsterdam was the centre of the sugar trade and rapidly became the centre for the spice trade for ships from the East and West Indies.

The firm of Bols International, now a huge international conglomerate, is one of the most important of the world's distillers and is still in production after four centuries. Bols still make geneva and, at the Bols Royal Distilleries, a range of superb liqueurs are also made to Lucas Bols' dictum "Do not mutilate Nature. Guide it to perfection."

Gin was first sold in England in chemists' shops.

Below: Dam Square, Amsterdam, 1659. Jacob van der Ulft (1627-89).

The Arrival of Distilling in England

In the last quarter of the 16th century the Netherlands became the battlefield of Europe as the armies of France, England and Spain fought over disputed territories. During the long drawn-out campaigns, both

*Left: The Effects of
Intemperance.
Jan Havicksz Steen
(1625-79).*

French and English soldiers were introduced to the
strong, distinctive tasting local grog. The French called it
genievre and the English *geneva* which was soon
shortened to *gin*. English soldiers and sailors took to this
new drink like babes to mother's milk and, by the time
the wars in Europe finally ended, they had brought the
taste for gin to England.

Spirits had been known in England since Tudor times
although they were rarely consumed. There are frequent
references in contemporary accounts of the early 17th
century to 'aquavitae', a crude distilled spirit which was
made from fermented grain, fruit, wine dregs or old cider.
In 1621 there were 200 establishments in the cities of
London and Westminster distilling aquavitae and 'other
strong and hott waters' mainly, it is supposed, for
medicinal purposes.

DUTCH COURAGE

*The term was first coined by
returning English soldiers
who had been much
impressed by the artificially
induced bravery
experienced by those who
had encountered Dutch
geneva during the war
against the French.*

At this time brandy was the favourite distilled spirit in England. Whisky was known and drunk only in Scotland and Ireland. It is important to remember that, unlike Ireland and Scotland, there was no established tradition of distilling spirits in England. The English had always relied on cheap imports of French brandy and had never developed large scale distilling concerns of their own.

The father of English distilling was Sir Theodore De Mayerne, a noted physician. In 1638 Sir Theodore was granted a patent for distilling 'strong waters'. In the same year, he and his friend, Thomas Cademan, physician to the Queen, founded The Company of Distillers. They obtained a Royal Charter conferring extensive powers on the Company and they drew up a list of regulations and recipes setting out the rules and standards of distillation, published as "The Distiller of London". Although gin was never specifically mentioned, it was Sir Theodore's insistence on the rectification of spirits and the Company's ban on the sale of 'low spirits' which was to later lead to the emphasis on quality in the production of spirits.

Throughout most of the 17th century, gin was distilled on a very small scale and it was produced chiefly as a

medicine. Soldiers and sailors were in on the secret however and the sea-ports were always a great centre for gin drinking.

BY ANY OTHER NAME

In the 17th century, gin in England also became known as Schiedam (after the distilling centre near Amsterdam) and Hollands. Although gin was not drunk widely, it was very well known in Plymouth, Bristol and Portsmouth, brought in by sailors travelling to Holland.

SAMUEL PEPYS AND GIN

In Pepys' famous diary, the entry of 10th October 1663 reads "Sir W. Batten did advise me to take some juniper water ....strong water made of juniper". Pepys, the foremost social commentator of his day and famous bon viveur, never refers to gin being drunk for pleasure, an indication that gin was not a social drink at the time.

One reason for the unpopularity of the Dutch was that in 1667, the year after the Great Fire in London, the Dutch Fleet had sailed boldly up the Thames and set fire to the English fleet in Chatham Dockyard.

Gin in England

Genever to Holland was, and to a certain extent still is, what whisky is to Scotland and vodka to Russia - the national drink. Given the unpopularity of the Dutch in England at this time, it seemed unlikely that a Dutch drink could ever replace the traditional English drinks of ale and beer or, further up the social scale, the popularity of French wine and brandy, but this is exactly what happened.

The turnaround in gin's fortunes began in 1689 with the 'Glorious Revolution'' which saw the ascent to the throne of William and Mary. Dutch Protestant William of Orange and his wife Mary, daughter of the deposed Catholic Stuart king, James II, were invited to take the British crown. James fled to France, landed in Ireland and fled again into exile at the court of Louis XIV after losing to William at the Battle of the Boyne.

The most immediate result of a Dutchman on the British throne was a complete reversal of traditional trading alliances. Everything French was out, all things Dutch were in. The drinking habits of centuries went through upheaval as Parliament, under William's influence, began to legislate against French imports of wine and brandy at the same time as encouraging the distillation of spirits from English grown corn.

This was popular with farmers who often had grain surpluses and sub-standard crops which they had been forced to sell at a loss, and which could now be sold at a profit to the emergent distilling industry.

Through her Stuart father Mary was directly descended from Mary, Queen of Scots. William of Orange could only claim the British throne by virtue of his marriage to her.

Protestants in Ireland are still known as Orangemen and the victory of Protestantism over Catholicism is celebrated in the Orange marches which take place every year in July.

The 1690 Act had been pushed through Parliament by a powerful combination of rich landowners and anti-French, anti-Catholic interests, many of whom had helped William to the throne. They wished to ensure that English agricultural interests were favoured.

William and Mary were violently anti-French. They themselves led the fashion for gin drinking by outlawing brandy and wine at Court in favour of the new spirit. It became a patriotic duty to drink gin, a sign of true Protestantism. This filtered down through society and for the first time the common people in England became spirits drinkers.

Legislating for Gin

The phenomenal growth of gin distilling in England at the beginning of the 18th century was a deliberate policy, greatly aided by various acts of legislation. The first of these was an Act of 1690 designed to encourage the

'distillation of brandy and spirits from corn'.

The provisions of the 1690 Act also negated the monopoly which had earlier been granted to the Worshipful Company of Distillers, allowing them sole rights to distil within London, Westminster and a 21 mile radius beyond.

From 1690 onwards, distilling was open to all. Anyone could invest in a small still and once a public notice of his intention to distil had been posted for at least ten days, he was free to make any amount of gin or other spirits he wanted.

The new industry was further helped by the raising of taxes on beer in 1694 so that gin actually became cheaper than beer.

In 1702 the remaining powers of the Distillers Company to control the quality of distillation were revoked.

The 1720 Mutiny Act excused tradesmen who were distillers from having soldiers billeted on them. Many more people turned to distilling as a way to avoid the unpopular task of providing food and shelter for the soldiers.

The unbridled licence allowed for by the new legislation opened a golden door of opportunity to many. Although it led to decades of excess and the misery of the Gin Era, it also resulted in the formation of one of Britain's great industries.

The 1690 act allowed for the free distillation of 'good and wholesome brandies, aquavitae and spirits, drawn and made from malted corn'. The choice of the word brandy was specifically directed against the French. The spirit produced was more like a rough whisky or schnapps and was sometimes known as "British brandy".

Gin could be made out of virtually any substance that would ferment and gin shops selling killer brews sprung up in every back street and alleyway. In 1721 a report of the Westminster justices stated that nowhere in London was there an area 'wherein the number of alehouses, brandy and geneva shops do not daily increase though they were so numerous already that ....every tenth house sells one sort or another of these liquors." This was optimistic as it is estimated that in slum areas like St. Giles one house in every four sold gin. On foggy nights even the air must have been intoxicating.

The Great Gin Binge

Gin drinking in England in the first part of the 18th century became an epidemic. In large cities like London, living and working conditions for the poor were appalling and gin provided a temporary escape from the grinding poverty and general hopelessness that was their lot. For the first time spirits were cheap, plentiful and available on almost every street corner. No wonder then that consumption went through the roof.

In 1689 the whole of England produced at most half a million gallons of gin a year. In 1727 the consumption of gin reached 5 million gallons. In 1733 London produced 11 million gallons of gin, 14 gallons for every adult

resident. And these were the official figures. They do not take into account the hundreds of illegal stills and shebeens producing home-made genever, a spirit which bore little resemblance to proper spirit and often had lethal effects.

There was little or no official control over either the production or sale of gin. By 1730 in London alone there were over 7,000 dram shops. Gin was sold everywhere: in taverns, alehouses and squalid gin shops, in chandler's merchants and corner stores, tobacconists, barbers, as well as by street hawkers and pedlars. Gin was available on every street and every street corner.

Drunk for 1d
Dead drunk for 2d
Straw for nothing
The notice put up by a publican in Southwark. The straw was for passing out on after over indulgence in often lethal and filthy brews.

ON THE SLATE

Gin was given to workers as part of their weekly wage. Unscrupulous employers sold gin to their workers on credit. By the end of the week many workers had no wages to collect and some would even have owed money.

Above left: Charter granted to Gordon's allowing them to distill gin.

Hogarth's Gin Lane is a graphic and compelling indictment of the perils of excessive gin drinking. Here the viewer is invited to consider its awful results - madness, suicide, death, neglect of children, abandonment and penury.

The Great Destroyer

The universal availability of cheap gin had dire results for the urban poor, of London especially. Whatever their route to the demon drink, they suffered the inevitable consequences - penury, ill-health, debt, crime and general despair. Some statistics give an idea of the extent of the problem:

In 1723 the death rate in London outstripped the birth rate and remained higher for the next ten years.

In the years 1730 to 1749, 75% of all the children christened in London were buried before the age of five.

Contemporary records speak of the hospices and hospitals in the City packed with 'increasing multitudes of dropsical and consumptive people arising from the effects of spirituous liquors'.

Not only were the hospitals full, the courts and gaols were full too of those for whom 'Gin alone was the cause of the transgression.... Gin is the principal sustenance (if it may be so called) of more than a hundred thousand people in the metropolis.' (Fielding: Essay *An Enquiry into the Causes of the Late Increase of Robbers.*)

Visitors to London spoke of scenes of squalor and public degradation with poor wretches lying drunk in the streets at all times of the day and night.

Clearly, although the drinking of spirits was not the only cause of misery amongst the poor, it played a major role in the social problems of the 18th century.

MOTHER'S RUIN

Between the years 1740 and 1742 in London there were two burials to every baptism in London. This statistic was laid at the door of gin which, it was thought, caused lower fertility, birth defects and poor parental care resulting in high infant mortality. Perhaps this is where the term 'mother's ruin' comes from.

Left: From a series of engravings by George Cruikshank.

THE REVEREND
JOHN TOWLEY'S
ATTACK ON GIN

Gin! cursed fiend with fury
fraught
Makes human race a prey,
It enters by a deadly
draught,
And steals our life away.

Virtue and truth, driven to
despair,
Its rages compel to fly,
But cherishes with hellish
care,
Theft, murder, perjury.

Dam'd cup that on the
vitals preys,
That liquid fire contains,
Which madness to the
heart conveys,
And rolls it through the
veins.

Attempts to Reform

From the late 1720s onwards there is evidence of the alarm the government was beginning to feel about the effect of gin on the health of the nation. Unfortunately the attempts made to introduce reforms were muddled, often producing the opposite effect to that intended.

• The Gin Act of 1729 required distillers to take out licences of £20 (a huge sum at the time) and pay excise tax of 2 shillings a gallon. The most immediate effect of this was an enormous increase in illicit distilling.

• In 1733 the Act of 1729 was repealed and replaced by legislation governing the sale of gin. No longer could street hawkers and shops sell spirits.

• The 1736 Gin Act fixed a licence fee of £50 for gin

sellers, prohibited the sale of gin in quantities of less than 2 gallons and put a tax of £1 a gallon on it. This law was intended to outlaw gin and was the result of a petition to Parliament brought by the magistrates of Middlesex who saw the effects of gin excess very clearly.

This Act caused serious unrest and riots. Walpole, then Prime Minister, claimed that the Jacobites were spreading sedition and inciting the common people to violence "at the approaching expiration of their darling vice".

COIN IN THE SLOT GIN

Captain Dudley Bradstreet, an enterprising informer turned bootlegger, took advantage of a loophole in the 1736 Act which stipulated that an informer must know the name of the owner of rented property from which illegal gin was sold. He promptly acquired a property whose ownership would prove difficult to establish and invested £13 in a stock of gin from Langdale's distillery in Holborn. He set up a trade sign depicting a cat and installed a slot and a lead pipe, one end of which was located under the cat's paw. To the other end, inside the house, he attached a funnel. His customers would arrive, place their money in the slot and duly receive their measures of gin from the cat's paw. His business prospered until competition became too stiff. As he recorded "My Scheme of Puss, now becoming common, was practised by many others, which greatly diminished my Business and made me drop it, and turn my Head to something else."

Madam Geneva rose from the grave very quickly. The provisions of the 1736 Act were easily evaded. A wine licence cost only a few shillings instead of £50, so many gin shops became 'wine merchants' overnight. Virtually the day after the Bill was passed, these were selling tots of what was essentially gin with a smattering of wine, called variously Sangaree, Tow-Row, Bob, Ladies Delight, Cuckolds Comfort, King Theodore of Corsica and Grape Waters. A Cockney wit christened the new brew - Parliamentary Brandy - a nickname that stuck.

More Attempts to Reform

The Act of 1736 was indeed extremely unpopular. As well as civil disorder all over the country, mock funerals with ceremonial processions for Madam Geneva took place the night before the Act became law. In the big cities, London, Plymouth, Bristol and Norwich the mob took to the streets determined to drown their sorrows in every drop of the last, legal cheap gin. It was one of the greatest binges ever and the next morning, not only was there a mass collective hangover, there was nothing left to drink.

In fact, this Act was almost unenforceable and sales of illicitly produced and sold gin soon rocketed. The Government was forced to repeal it in 1742.

In 1743 the Government introduced yet another Gin Act. This time licences of £1 to sell gin were to be granted to the holders of beer and ale licences and distillers were not allowed to retail gin direct to the public but only to licensed houses. This was obviously a more sensible law, badly needed, given that in this year, London produced 20 million gallons of gin which was mostly sold to its 500,000 population.

THIS is the *Landlord* who coins his bright gold,
Out of the ruin of youthful and old,
Who drink the strong liquors he sells night and day,
At the bar of the Gin-shop, so glittering and gay.

Between 1736 and 1743 only two of the £50 retail licences were acquired yet the quantity of spirits consumed soared to a new high. The Act also encouraged paid informers and, between September 1736 and July 1738, 12,000 informations were made against spirits sellers. It was a dangerous occupation as informers were universally loathed, often attacked and occasionally murdered. And, although 12,000 were convicted the number of penalty fines actually paid was negligible.

The custodians and those who worked in gaols and work-houses were often only marginally better off than the inmates of these establishments. They depended on the sale of alcohol to boost their meagre earnings and were furious when this source of income was removed.

The End of The Gin Era

The benefit of the Act of 1743 was to have created a strategy which remains to this day - to make the sale of gin public and therefore respectable, and to increase the price of spirits. Rather than try to introduce a form of prohibition which could not be enforced, the Government tried to encourage moderation which turned out to be a far more successful policy.

Popular opinion had been much affected by the publication in 1750 of Hogarth's Gin Lane and of Henry Fielding's Enquiry in 1751. Spurred on by a rising anti-gin crusade, Parliament passed a law in 1751, known as the Tippling Act, which placed further controls on those licensed to retail gin. Only established licensed public houses were now legally entitled to sell gin. If credit was given to customers, sums under £1 were not recoverable in law. In addition chandlers and those in charge of gaols and poor-houses were specifically forbidden to retail spirits.

By further controlling those who could legally retail gin and by raising excise duties, the Act wiped out the advantages gin had enjoyed for 60 years. Gin was no longer cheap, nor easily available. Effective legislation also led to proper supervision of distilling and encouraged respectable firms to become involved. It is no coincidence that the rise of the great distilling concerns dates from this time.

This is the *woman*, with wobegone face,
The wife of the drunkard, in rags and disgrace,
Who is served by the lady, all jewels and lace,
The wife of the landlord who coins his bright gold,
Out of the ruin of youthful and old,
Who drink the strong liquors he sells night and day,
At the bar of the Gin-shop, so glittering and gay.

GIN - THE HEALTHY ALTERNATIVE

Not only was gin cheap and available it was also safer to drink than either water or milk. Milk in the 17th and 18th centuries was a complete health hazard. It was either brought in from farms on the outskirts of towns or came from cows who were kept in filthy conditions in backstreets. In either case by the time it reached the household it was often sour and diseased. The development of the railways made it possible to bring milk into towns by train and improve the quality and freshness of the milk considerably.

Water was often not much better. A pamphlet of 1827 declared that inhabitants of Westminster were supplied with water 'in a state Offensive to the Sight, Disgusting to the Imagination and Injurious to the Health'. Water-borne diseases contributed greatly to an average expectation of life of only 30 years.

Discovering Gin

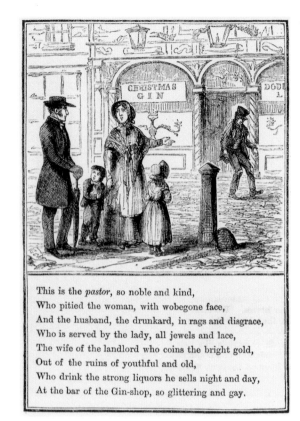

This is the pastor, so noble and kind,
Who pitied the woman, with wobegone face,
And the husband, the drunkard, in rags and disgrace,
Who is served by the lady, all jewels and lace,
The wife of the landlord who coins the bright gold,
Out of the ruins of youthful and old,
Who drink the strong liquors he sells night and day,
At the bar of the Gin-shop, so glittering and gay.

Another factor to impact on the price of gin was that, in years of bad harvest as in 1757, 1759 and 1760 the distillation of corn from spirits was prohibited. Prices immediately shot up and consumption fell correspondingly. Parliament was besieged with petitions demanding that the prohibition should be permanent. The farmers naturally protested their case. In the end however Parliament decided that the high price of spirits had greatly benefited ordinary people and immediately raised the duty again.

There is no doubt that the impetus for reform was a genuine reaction to the excesses of the gin era. However Parliament had also quickly caught on to the fact that raising the tax and duties on gin produced a valuable source of revenue for the public purse. Unfortunately for spirits drinkers this has been an example that successive Chancellors of the Exchequer have been eager to follow. Killjoy budgets have been a feature of all Parliaments since.

However the policy did succeed. By the end of the 18th century gin was no longer the opium of the masses and the principal reason was expense. The excise duty on spirits had risen from £7 7s 0d in 1751 to £61 19s 9d in

1791. To all intents and purposes, the worst aspects of the gin problem were priced out of existence.

Gin did not go away and once the social stigma of the gutter began to be removed, it was free to develop into the distinctive and sophisticated drink it is today.

Londoners revived the memory of the days of cheap gin when, during the Gordon Riots of 1780, the London mob gutted the Langdale distilleries in Holborn. The reason for the attack was that Langdale was a Catholic but the rabble were soon helping themselves to free gin. Describing the drunken scenes outside the distillery Walpole wryly commented "As yet there are more persons killed by drinking than by ball or bayonet.

Many of London's coffee houses survive today as gentlemen's clubs. St. James, Whites and Boodles are amongst the best known. Lloyds, the insurance giant, started life as a coffee house as did the Stock Exchange where they do business 'on the floor of the House' and the attendants are still referred to as 'waiters'.

PART III: GIN IN THE 19TH CENTURY

Well into Victorian times attitudes to drinking and drunkenness were quite different from modern attitudes which have been much influenced by the ideas of the temperance movement. Spirits were generally drunk by all classes and ages of the population not least because drinking either water or milk was dangerous. Alcohol was supposed to impart strength and vigour. Invalids and nursing mothers were prescribed spirits to thicken their blood and restore their energies and those who worked outdoors drank spirits to keep out the cold.

Once the days of cheap gin disappeared, drinking habits throughout the country became far more moderate. An American visitor to London in 1805 commented, "the

common people in England drink but little ardent spirits because its excessive dearness places it almost beyond their reach ......in our country the effects are dreadful because every man can procure it."

The Napoleonic Wars introduced a degree of sobriety to the nation and, certainly amongst the middle classes, drunkenness was increasingly viewed as socially unacceptable. More importantly for the cause of sobriety, from the 1820s to the 1850s there was a huge rise in coffee and tea drinking. There were established coffee houses which had always catered for the professional classes but now that prices had fallen to within their reach, working men began to enjoy coffee and tea.

When tea first arrived in London in the middle of the 17th century, it sold for the huge sum of £3.50 per pound. As exports from the Empire grew, prices tumbled leading to a massive rise in consumption. For example, in the 19th century, tea consumption rose from 1.6lb per person in the decade 1841-50 to 5.7 lbs in 1891-1900.

In contrast to spirits, beer drinking was seen as socially acceptable and morally upright. Hogarth's companion piece to Gin Lane was Beer Town where all is order, calm and sobriety.

Later on, beer was seen as a temperance drink and any attacks on drunkenness were made against spirit-drinking.

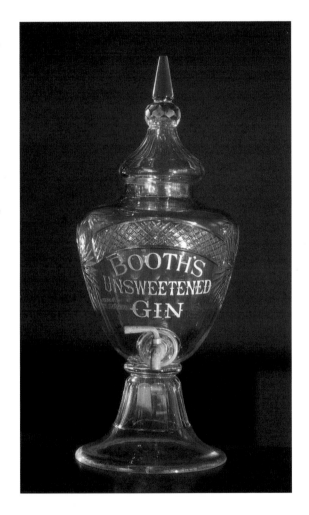

Right: Early Branded bar dispenser

At the lower end of the social scale, excessive drinking, although nothing like on the scale seen 50 years before, remained a feature of working class life.

The Government had encouraged the brewing and consumption of beer at the expense of spirits and by 1836 there was a total of 56,000 beer shops in England and Wales. Rather like the gin situation 100 years earlier, a licence to sell beer was cheap and duties on beer low. Beer again became the favourite tipple of the poor.

Some brewers sought to protect the interests of their tied houses by building new, luxurious premises designed to entice passing traffic. To compete with the new beer-houses, gin-shops acquired additional premises to sell their more expensive spirits. These were magnificent - shining edifices of mirrors and glass, lavishly fitted out with blazing fires and comfortable furnishings, staffed by friendly, jolly barmaids. Like a fantastical stage set the gin palace had appeared.

The first gin palace to open in London was probably that of Fearon's in Holburn Hill in about 1830.

Charles Dickens in his role of social commentator gives a much quoted contemporary description of a gin palace:
"You turn the corner. What a change All is light and brilliancy. The hum of many voices issues from that splendid gin-shop which forms the commencement of the two streets opposite; and the gay building with the fantastically ornamented parapet, the illuminated clock, the plate-glass windows surrounded by stucco rosettes, and its profusion of gas-lights in richly-gilt burners, is perfectly dazzling when contrasted with the dirt and dark we have just left. The interior is even gayer than the exterior. A bar of French-polished mahogany,

Palaces of the People

Some idea of the splendour of Victorian gin palaces can be gleaned by visiting such glorious relicts of the past as The Duke of Clarence in London, The Crown in Belfast, The Cafe Royal in Edinburgh or The Horseshoe in Glasgow. These marvellous Victorian pubs have retained much of their original design and contrast starkly with the canned music, and gimcrack decor of their modern descendants.

Victorian gin palaces sold a variety of beers and spirits as well as gin and soon there were thousands of them throughout the country. They were oases of glamour in deserts of squalid uniformity and were immensely popular with the public.

elegantly-carved, extends the whole width of the place; and there are two side-aisles of great casks, painted green and gold, and bearing such inscriptions as 'Old Tom, 549'; 'Young Tom, 360'; 'Samson, 1421' the figures agreeing, we presume, with 'gallons'. Beyond the bar is a lofty and spacious saloon, full of the same enticing vessels, with a gallery running round it, equally well furnished."

Gin palaces were open to all. They were warm, cosy and brightly lit. They offered company and a common meeting place sorely missed by the many city workers who had left secure village communities to come and work in the new factories. Where the gin-shops of the previous century had been squalid hovels and the alehouses more of a home from home, the gin palace provided an escape from home.

For many the gin palace was the sole centre of recreation and moreover, it was a glamorous and exciting place where ordinary working people could feel like kings and queens. All for the price of a tot of gin or a pint of porter.

Old Tom is a sweet, heavy gin which all distillers used to produce. It gradually went out of favour as dry gin became more established and by the 1920s, demand for Old Tom was falling off although Gordon's produced an Old Tom gin into the 1970s. Its decrease in popularity was no doubt due to the fact that Old Tom did not mix well. Old Tom was the gin of 18th century England and some idea of what it tasted like can be had from sampling a modern Dutch genever. No-one can explain the name. There is a story that a cat fell accidentally into the still and so improved the flavour that it was thereafter called Old Tom.

Upwards Mobile

The gin palace helped make gin a more respectable drink and it began to gain ground, even social acceptance, amongst the middle classes. Partly this was due to the dramatic increase in the quality of gin available.

London had become a centre for gin distilling. The fledgling industry was dominated by a small group of families - the Booths, the Gilbeys, Gordons, Tanquerays - who gave their names to leading brands of gin still enjoyed today. Although Booth's is probably the oldest brand still in existence closely followed by Gordon's, by the 1830s there were a number of fine distillers with a reputation for superior products prospering in London. As the power of the distilling concerns grew, so too did the prestige of gin.

The invention of the continuous still by Aeneas Coffey in 1832 had allowed for a purer

GORDON & Co.;
Distillers & Wine Merchants,
132, GOSWELL ROAD, LONDON.

GORDIAN LIST.

		Strength.		Per Gall.
15-	Aniseed	32.0	...	12/6
77-	do.	7	...	8/-
7c	do.	7	...	6/6
	ange Bitters	40.0	...	10/6
62	do.	60.0	...	8/-
63	Cherry Bra y (Morella)	60.0	...	14/-
43-0	Clove	50.0	...	10/-
62	do.	60.0	...	8/-
41-0	Creme d'Orange	40.0	...	12/6
31-0	Ginger Brandy	32.0	...	13/-
63-0	do.	60.0	...	8/6
43-0	Ginger Gin	40.0	...	12/-
77-0	Gingerette	70.0	...	8/-
73-0	Lovage	70.0	...	8/-
83-0	Milk Punch	60.0	per doz.	28/-
33-0	Noyeau	50.0	...	11/-
67-0	do.	60.0	...	9/-
33-0	Orange Brandy	50.0	...	14/-
63-0	Mint	60.0	...	9/6
77-0	do.	70.0	...	7/6
70-0	do.	78.0	...	5/6
67-0	Raspberry	65.0	...	10/-
73-0	Rum Shrub	70.0	...	10/-
89-0	do.	75.0	...	8/-
	Sloe Gin	45.0 0	...	10/6

Left: Early Gordon & Co. cordials list.

Distillers and maltsters used to keep pigs as a side-line feeding them the left-overs of the grain after malting and distilling. One of the reasons for London's pre-eminence in distilling was the purity and reliable supply of the water to be found in its (then) outlying villages, like Clerkenwell (Clerk's Well) where Alexander Gordon established his distillery in 1769. Booth's also had chosen its location to draw on the pure water from the Finsbury spa which was chosen to reduce the spirit.

spirit of quality to be produced and also guaranteed consistency of product. These two factors contributed greatly to gin's enhanced reputation.

Some 18th century distilling families have long since been forgotten. Not so the family of Israel Wilkes, a London distiller who was the father of John Wilkes, the radical politician. John Wilkes emigrated to America and Wilkes Bar in Pennsylvania is named after him. His cousin Elizabeth Wilkes married a Booth and founded the famous Booth acting family. It was her descendant, John Wilkes Booth, who assassinated President Lincoln.

London Dry is a generic term for gin which is unsweetened, dry and less aromatic. Although by law London Dry can be made anywhere, in some countries the description is only allowed if the gin is imported from the UK. World-wide, London Dry gin made in the UK is still considered the best.

The increasing popularity of unsweetened gin over the highly flavoured, sweet, traditional gins established a fashion for what became known as London Dry. The first London Drys were stronger in flavour than most modern gins but far more sophisticated than the old-fashioned gins which tasted more like cordials. Soon every major distiller was producing a version of London Dry. There were variations between each brand according to the different formulae

SPECIAL

LONDON

DRY GIN

ENGLAND

used in production and, as with wines and brandy, customers developed preferences for one or another brand.

The new London Dry gin was a very different drink from the old rot-gut sold in the alleyways of the East End. It was a complex drink whose subtleties appealed to a more sophisticated palate. The success of the London Dry style of gin had enormous impact on gin's status. For the first time in its eventful history gin acquired class and became a drink for the respectable drinker.

A large scale reorganisation of the distilling industry in London with firms like Gordon's and Tanqueray joining forces in 1898 had resulted in further improvements to the quality of gin.

In the 1890s gin began to be sold in bottles as a response to a growing demand from the middle classes to buy their gin in bottles to take home. The first gin bottles were dark green and more elongated in shape than modern ones. They were copies of bottles imported from Holland. Later bottles were made of clear glass and came about as a direct result of the export trade and consumers' mistrust of goods that had travelled long distances. They wanted to see what they were buying. Gordon's still sells gin for the home market in distinctive dark green bottles retaining the clear glass version for export gin.

Gin's Increasing Respectability

Gin found an appreciative audience amongst middle-class women who either belonged to society or aspired to belong to society. Part of its charm was that it was perceived as an elegant drink, made even more attractive by the fact that it looked like water and had very little smell. Genteel ladies coyly called gin 'white wine' and were no doubt extremely glad that it could be bought at the local grocers instead of in a disreputable gin shop.

Gin had always had naval associations and Pink Gin was a traditional navy drink. For medical reasons naval officers

were obliged to take regular doses of a tincture made from the bark of the Angostura tree found in South America. Some naval genius had discovered how well the angostura or 'bitters' complemented gin and passed on the method for making 'pink' gin - shake the thick angostura drops into a glass, coat the glass with the essence, shake out the excess and add gin. According to navy tradition a proper Pink Gin is one that is made with Plymouth Gin which has a very distinctive flavour.

Retired naval officers carried on imbibing their favourite tipple and introduced the fashion for this popular mixed drink.

Nig
Some Victorian decanter labels bore the word 'nig'. Whether this was extreme Victorian prudery, a hypocritical attempt to deceive children and servants or Cockney slang, no-one knows.

GIN PIAJ
In India the addition of tiny onions which have been marinated in chilli transforms a pink gin into a Gin Piaj.

In the UK gin is drunk far more widely by women than by men whilst in the United States gin drinking is equal between the sexes. Pink Gin has always remained very much a man's drink. Perhaps this is because angostura has a reputation as a very effective aphrodisiac. Not something you would imagine sailors on three month voyages without a port of call would need.

SIR FELIX BOOTH

Sir Felix was an unusual character. A successful businessman, he was also a philanthropist. In 1829 he anonymously donated £20,000 to finance an expedition to Canada to search for a north-west passage from the Atlantic to the Pacific. The expedition was led by his friend and protégé, Captain John Ross and was a disaster. Having been given up for dead, it was rescued in the spring of 1833 and returned in October 1833. All was not lost as Captain Ross's nephew, James Clark Ross located the true position of the North Magnetic Pole. He marked the spot with a Union Jack and celebrated with Booth's gin. In the course of his wandering

Export Gin

Gin's respectability was further increased as the servants of the Raj and other colonial outposts returned home with their gin drinking habit intact.

Until the mid-19th century all UK produced gin was for the domestic market. Excise duties made gin too expensive to export and the Government were inflexibly determined to extract every penny of duty, much to the chagrin of the large distillers.

In 1850, Sir Felix Booth of the Booth distilling family, with great foresight, spent a considerable amount of money on getting a Private Bill through Parliament which was to remove excise duties on gin manufactured for export.

Immediately vast new markets for gin were opened. A thirsty world was waiting for English gin which had already established a fine reputation for quality. Gordon's export order books show a request for a quantity of gin from a group of Australian settlers who sent their payment in advance - in gold dust. Today gin is a huge export industry with over 25 million litres of gin exported to 185 countries.

Gin developed a mixed reputation in parts of Africa where large amounts were exported in the late 19th century by the Germans and the English. This was because although the English sent their best quality gin for export the Germans off-loaded inferior gin on to the export market.

Ross had named huge areas of land and sea after his benefactor and maps of the area still rather bizarrely show Boothia peninsula, Felix Harbour, Cape Felix, the Gulf of Boothia and Boothia Isthmus.

In 1860 gin and soda with a slice of lemon was known as the 'British soldier's delight.'

In 1806 an American journal "The Balance" gave this description of a cocktail "Cocktail is a stimulating liquor composed of spirits of any kind, sugar, water and bitters - it is vulgarly called bittered sling and is supposed to be an excellent electioneering potion."

The first American unsweetened (dry) gin was produced in Ohio by the Fleischman brothers who established their distillery in 1870.

A New Outlook for a New Century

At the turn of the century two other developments further consolidated gin's upward mobility. The first of these was the effects of the phylloxera plague which had ravaged Europe since the 1860s. Phylloxera was a fungus disease which affected vines causing them to rot and wither. It caused havoc, destroying thousands of hectares of vines until a way was found to transplant healthy vines from the New World on to European stock. The disease had a major effect on English drinking habits in that brandy became almost unobtainable. Although many spirits drinkers turned to whisky, many

Right: Labelling the early pre-mixed cocktail shakers.

also discovered a taste for gin and stuck to it even after brandy became generally available again.

Left: Gordon's messenger in uniform.

The arrival of a new type of American traveller who introduced the concept of cocktails to Britain was also influential. Sophisticated upper class Americans, as personified in the novels of Henry James, came to London and other European cities as part of the 19th century equivalent of the Grand Tour. They brought with them the new fashion for drinking cocktails.

The first reference to the word 'cocktail' in English literature is found in "Tom Brown's Schooldays". In this novel by the great Victorian moralist, Matthew Arnold, Flashman the villain drinks gin punch whilst the other boys drink beer.

Cocktail drinking in America was given an added boost with the introduction of ready mixed proprietary cocktails. Heublein's of Hartford, Connecticut were manufacturing these in 1892. Their first product was a gin mix which consisted of gin, red vermouth and other flavourings. Advertising was very sophisticated and obviously aimed at women.

The etymology of the word 'cocktail' has provoked much controversy. Here are some possible explanations:

- *Cocktail - from the habit of docking the tails of horses of impure stock*

- *'Cock-àle' was a mixture of spirits fed to fighting cocks which would also be drunk by those who won the bet with the number of tail feathers in the drink supposedly displaying the number of ingredients in the drink*

The Early Days of the Cocktail

Whilst mixed drinks had always been popular in America and in Victorian England, in America in the 19th century the cocktail was invented. Its fame soon spread.

A well-known American bartender, Jerry Thomas, had published a book in the mid-19th century called the *Bon Vivant's Guide or How to Mix Drinks* which gave hundreds of recipes for cocktails. This was followed in 1882 by Harry Johnson who published his *Bartender's Manual or How to Mix Drinks of the Present Style*. Both make fascinating reading with drinks and names for cocktails that

Right: Gordon's senior managers at play.

have completely disappeared.

In Britain traditionally cocktails were drunk at picnics or at other outdoor events, very rarely at formal social occasions. The cups, punches, toddies, flips, fizzes, slings of Victorian England all qualify as cocktails and there is no better proof of the improvement in gin's social image than the recipes for Mint Julep and Gin Sling included in the 1894 edition of Mrs. Beeton's famous cookery book.

In the 1860s a bar was opened by an American behind the Bank of England which served such wonderfully bracing concoctions as the Connecticut Eye-Opener and the Alabama Fog-Cutter. In 1891 the first true cocktail bar, the Criterion, opened in London introducing the joys of the cocktail to a far wider audience.

- *In Bordeaux 'un coqutel' was a mixed drink and the word could have passed into English through French officers serving in the American War of Independence*
- *Xochitl - an Aztec princess who beguiled her king with a drink of her own devising*

Right from the start there was disagreement between those who believed in temperance, which allowed beer and wine to be drunk, and those who believed in abstinence from all alcoholic drink. The use of the word teetotaller came from the taking of the pledge in 1833 by Dicky Turner, who got so carried away with enthusiasm, he started stammering and vowed to t-t-t-t-totally give up drink. Joseph Livesy, the leader of the abstinence movement instantly adopted teetotal as a name for the movement. From then on abstainers were known as teetotallers.

PART IV: THE PROHIBITION YEARS
The Temperance Movement in Britain

One of the reasons why Victorian England never experienced the epidemic of drunkenness of the century before was the presence of a vociferous, powerful and organised anti-drink lobby.

The temperance movement began in the United States and, by the 1830s, temperance ideas were gaining hold in Britain. In Britain however, the temperance movement never achieved the real political power it did in the United States and certainly never succeeded in outlawing spirits, or banning all alcoholic drinks. It did however have an influence which was quite out of proportion to its numbers and was instrumental in securing legislation to control when, how and by whom alcohol could be sold.

A significant part of why the prohibitionists failed in Britain was the uniquely British fundamental belief in the freedom of the individual summed up by a bishop's declaration during the licensing debate in the House of Lords "I would rather see England free than England sober".

To this unshakeable conviction was added the weight of the prestige and power of the drinks industry which by the turn of the century was formidable.

"To the poor and unlettered drink stands in the place of symphony concerts and of literature" William James. This was a sentiment that even Victorian reformers understood which was one reason why the prohibition movement happily never achieved the power it did in the United States

When the Liberal government went to the country in 1874, it was decisively rejected by the voters who had not forgotten Gladstone's attempts to interfere with their right to drink. "We have been borne down in a torrent of gin...." wrote Gladstone.

The wealth and prestige of the drinks industry was enormous between 1892 and 1912. During this time, 9 brewers, 2 distillers, 1 malster and 1 wine merchant all died leaving over a £1,000,000 - a truly fabulous sum at the time.

The first pledge to abstain from spirits was made at a meeting in New York in 1808 and the first pledge to abstain completely in Boston in 1826.

Prohibition in America - The Noble Experiment

Although there had been many efforts over the years to curtail the manufacture and sale of strong liquor, especially gin, none of these attempts had ever been successful.

Only in the United States of the 20th century was a 'noble experiment' to completely eliminate gin and other alcoholic drinks to be seriously attempted.

Prohibition had its roots in the temperance movements which had started in the 18th century America. By the 19th century the temperance groups had gathered real impetus. Not surprising when one considers the leading role that strong drink had played in American society since the first colonists had arrived.

The 19th century was a carousing century with all the social classes imbibing freely. In the South a mint julep was a breakfast drink whilst slaves and servants knocked back a lethal combination of gin and applejack. Even babies were hardened spirits drinkers with rum and opium commonly used as a sedative.

By 1834 there were 1 million members of temperance societies out of a population of 13 million. In 1851 the State of Maine became the first state to ban the sale of liquor and throughout most of the 19th century there continued to exist 'wet' and 'dry' states.

A Kentucky woman, Carrie Nation, was the most fanatic of the prohibitionists. Her confrontational methods involved storming into saloons and smashing them up with a hatchet. The press adored her and she developed an effective public relations strategy. She would often smash saloons to suit a photo opportunity and had little souvenir hatchets made to distribute to her admirers. Her violence frightened others in the movement who tried to disown her. She never lived to see the triumph of prohibition dying in 1911 of muscular paralysis.

The two most famous Prohibition agents were characters called Moe and Izzy who adopted a variety of unusual disguises to trap their prey and had a reputation for always getting their man.

The reformers realised that only by adopting 'dry' legislation nationwide would it be possible to enforce it effectively. From 1914 onwards therefore, prohibition was their goal.

In 1917 Congress adopted the 18th Amendment which would introduce national prohibition. The Amendment was turned into law by the Volstead Act which made it a crime to manufacture or sell any beverage containing more that 0.5% alcohol (the weakest alcoholic drink contains about 2.5% alcohol).

THE FRUITS OF TEMPERANCE.

"Behold the son of Temperance, with buoyant heart and step, returning to his home; the partner of his bosom looks up and evinces his welcome; his children fly to meet him, their little arms embrace him, and with lip and heart they bless him."

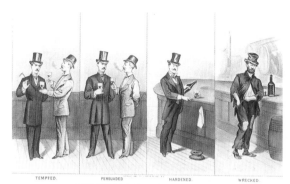

TEMPTED.   PERSUADED.   HARDENED.   WRECKED.

THE PROGRESS OF INTEMPERANCE.

The Prohibition law was the work of Wayne Wheeler, a senior member of the Anti-Saloon League founded in 1893. The League was an extremely powerful force in American politics and was successful in getting 'dry' candidates elected and 'dry' legislation enacted. Its methods were straightforward: it threatened all candidates for election with the loss of the dry vote unless they supported the League.

On January 17th 1920 the Volstead Act came into force and the biggest, most expensive surprise party in the world got going.

With the benefit of hindsight, it seems extraordinary naiveté on the part of the reformers to imagine that it would be possible to enforce this draconian law. The Act provided for a Prohibition Unit to be established within the Bureau of Internal Revenue. To this Unit were assigned 1,500 Prohibition agents, all paid a miserly salary of 2,000 dollars. Neither in numbers or motivation were they to prove effective law enforcers as the Government was to find out.

Even in the dry states there was no law against giving away drink which led to much local entrepreneurial spirit. A fine example was the clever gent who acquired a blind pig, set it up in a small enclosure and posted a sign "Look at the Blind Pig - Ten Cents a Look" Naturally with every look he gave away a free dram.

Those rich enough to avoid Prohibition did so. It was not illegal to supply alcohol that had been purchased before the Act came into force and the Yale Club, for example laid down enough stocks to last for fourteen years.

The immediate results of the Volstead Act were utterly predictable. Thousands of homes were transformed into miniature distilleries and breweries. Speak-easies selling unbelievably bad gin sprung up in every back street. Millions of ordinary law-abiding American citizens became criminals overnight. When the law caught up with offenders, harsh sentences were often passed, as in the case of the mother of ten in Michigan who was sentenced

Al Capone

to life imprisonment for possessing a pint of gin.

Meanwhile the law was either blind or powerless when it came to organised crime which was the true beneficiary of the Prohibition years. Men like Al Capone, Jack Diamond and Dutch Schultz emerged from poor, tough backgrounds to make fortunes and found empires of crime which were to last long after Prohibition.

It is estimated that, during Prohibition, the American population spent an average of 4,000 million dollars a year on illicit alcohol. In one single year the US consumed:

- 206 million gallons of hard liquor
- 684 million gallons of malt liquor
- 108 million gallons of wine

Perhaps the American public had followed the example of Groucho Marx who famously claimed "I was T-T until Prohibition."

Speak-easies selling illicit alcohol sprang up all over America. Some were rough shacks, close cousins of the gin-shops of 18th century London. Others were glamorous night-clubs where people went to drink, eat and listen to jazz. In New York alone there were an estimated 32,000 speak-easies, a great many of them owned and operated by gangsters.

*In 1925, five years after the
introduction of Prohibition,
Chicago with a population
of 3 million had 16,000
more arrests for
drunkenness than the whole
of England and Wales with
a population of 40 million.*

Bathtub Gin

Just two short years after Prohibition was introduced,
private stocks of liquor had begun to run out and America
entered the era of home brewed gin and whisky which
probably did more damage than any that has ever resulted
from drink being freely available.

It was soon discovered that you could make alcohol
from practically anything and many people simply made
their own. There were a number of vicious brews in
general circulation, many of which caused blindness,

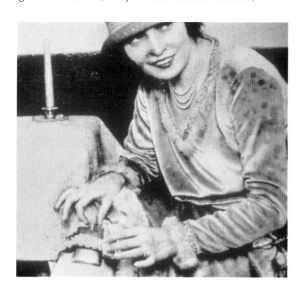

*Right: There were few
extents to which drinkers
would not go during
prohibition.*

hysteria, coma and even death. True bathtub gin was probably the most lethal and was produced by adding water, mineral oil and juniper juice to industrial alcohol. The Government tried to stop its manufacture by adding poisons to the industrial alcohol. This did not deter people from drinking it even when the death toll rose alarmingly and there was a national outcry.

Professional distillers who had been producing moonshine illegally for years upped production, making large quantities of illegal spirits for distribution to the bootleggers. Some of it was of reasonable quality. Very soon the large gangs moved in on the distilling business and set up properly run, large scale distilleries whose products reached the public through a complex web of bribery, intimidation and corruption.

Jazz came of age during Prohibition. The whole area around 35th Street in Chicago was a warren of cheap, sawdust-floored speak-easies humming with jazz. It was said that the air was so rich in music, that if you held up an instrument, the breeze would play a tune. There were casualties too - like the golden boy of jazz, Bix Beiderbecke, who died in 1931 at the age of 28 from the effects of bootleg gin.

Mary MacCarthy, the American novelist describes how, as a young student during Prohibition, she and a group of friends were touring around, staying at hotels and ordering gin from the bell-boys. Driving to Helena they had a bottle of moonshine and were drinking from it as they drove. Drops spilled on to her leg which she ignored. It was only when she arrived at their destination and was changing for dinner that she noticed that there were holes burnt in her stockings where the drops of 'gin' had spilled. The next bottle of gin they bought made them even more suspicious and, when they had it analysed, it was found to contain wood alcohol which could have killed them.

During the First World War there were shortages of all alcoholic drinks. Gin had received a boost as a result of the legislation brought in by the British Government to curb the sales of grain whisky which, it was considered, was affecting wartime productivity. All grain whisky had to be aged for a minimum period of 3 years. Gin, as a re-distilled spirit, did not. Many drinkers of grain whisky turned to gin.

English Gin and Prohibition

At first it seemed that Prohibition would have a disastrous effect on the English distilling trade. The United States was, indeed still is, the biggest market for the export of English gin. Before Prohibition was declared London companies were exporting large quantities of gin and Gordon's, one of the major distillers, had already begun distilling in the US.

However despite the predictions of gloom, there remained a number of people who were prepared to pay

The Real McCoy
The expression came from the exploits of Captain Bill McCoy, who ran liquor in from the eastern seaboard and who was famous for the quality of his liquor and his honesty.

whatever it cost for imported English gin because they appreciated its superior quality. Throughout Prohibition London distilleries continued to export large amounts (an official estimate of 40 million dollars worth) to the United States via Canada, the West Indies and tiny islands just off America's eastern seaboard. No questions were ever asked even when one company received an order for an enormous consignment of gin, cash in advance, from an island with a minute population. The order also specified that each case of the consignment be packaged in such a way that it could float.

English gin entered the US in various ways - over the border from Canada or Mexico or in boats from the smugglers' offshore bases - despite the best efforts of American coastguard and customs officials to prevent them. Not even the deployment of 20 naval destroyers was able to stop the smugglers.

Although nowadays the United States has many distilleries making very good quality gin and many large English distillers operating under licence, it is still the biggest market for imported English gin. American customers will specify their favourite brand by name when ordering a drink in a bar.

Bootlegging was a highly profitable activity and many people became involved as a contemporary song showed:

> *"Mother makes brandy from cherries*
> *Pop distils whisky and gin;*
> *Sister sells wine from the grapes on our vine -*
> *Good grief how the money rolls in".*

Below: The Real McCoy 'Bill McCoy'.

In 1931 Hoover appointed a commission to enquire into prohibition. Its report was confused and contradictory and was greeted with derision by the press and public alike. Franklin P. Adams' little poem summed up the mood:

"Prohibition is an awful flop.
We like it.
It can't stop what it's meant to stop.
We like it.
It's left a trail of graft and slime,
And it don't prohibit worth a dime.
It's filled our land with vice and crime,
Nevertheless, we're for it".

The End of Prohibition

By 1930 Prohibition was quite clearly unenforceable: even the police had given up trying. As America moved into a period of deep economic depression there was public resentment against the illicit wealth that had been created and the antics of the millionaire gangsters who had profited on such a huge scale. Led by a group of society women who were tired of their families being turned into criminals and United States law being made a fool of, the movement against Prohibition swung into action.

On the 5th December 1933 Utah became the thirty-sixth state to ratify the repeal of Prohibition. As the news came over the air, America was poised, cocktail shaker in hand to celebrate the end of this absurd law which had caused so much misery and done so much harm.

For the cost of the experiment had been high - $5,000 million in lost revenues, $500 million in pointless enforcement efforts, not to mention the lives and health of thousands of ordinary Americans. More than anything else, Prohibition had established corruption and bribery as a feature of public life. Worst of all, it had been directly responsible for the birth of organised crime.

One thing that America learned during those thirteen years was that alcohol was a part of civilised life. After Repeal of the Act the demand for English gin was much larger than it had been before because the reputation of London Dry gin had never been higher.

Occasionally American prohibitionists would try to preach their gospel in Britain. One of the most famous of these misguided evangelists was W. E. 'Pussyfoot' Johnson. Sadly his mission to convert the English came to an abrupt halt when he was kidnapped by medical students from King's College in London. They paraded him through the streets to a tune of their own devising.

"Mr. Pussyfoot, miaow-wow
Mr. Pussyfoot, miaow-wow
Fancy coming from America to try
To make Old England dry

Uncle Sam stood it like a lamb,
But if you think we are going to allow
Any crank of a Yank to put us in a water tank -
Mr. Pussyfoot, miaow-wow".

The cocktail party was introduced to London by an American-born hostess called Madame Alfredo de Pena in the late 1920s.

PART V: THE COCKTAIL YEARS
The Cocktail Craze

COCKTAIL DRESS
To keep pace with the cocktail craze fashion designers and dress shops produced cocktail dresses to be worn at cocktail parties. Generally they were short, stylish and quite simple in design.

Cocktails had been around since Victorian times but in Europe and the United States in the 1920s they became a craze, giving rise to the term, the Cocktail Age.

There were many reasons why cocktails became so popular. The first was practical: much of the gin and whisky available during Prohibition was so bad that it was practically undrinkable. The taste of bathtub gin could be disguised by adding other drinks and mixes and so during Prohibition literally thousands of cocktails were invented. Many of them crossed the Atlantic on board the huge liners sailing from New York and soon in Europe cocktails began to represent fun, glamour and having a good time.

   The second reason was sociological and applied more in Britain. After the Great War there was an unwillingness to return to the extreme social formality of the pre-War years. Formal dinners for which one was required to 'dress' were no longer the norm and the simple fact was no-one quite knew what to do in the hours between 6pm and 8pm. So the cocktail hour came into being and, with the cocktail hour, came the cocktail party. Everyone was giving parties and experimenting with new cocktails and, because gin was the base for many of them, it became the star of the Cocktail Age.

Alec Waugh, in his book "Merchants of Wine' describes a conversation with the painter C.R.W Nevinson and his wife. Because there was nothing to do in London between tea and dinner the Nevinsons had thought it a good idea to have a party and serve cocktails. They duly invited thirty people and were surprised when only two guests showed up. Clearly the novelty of going to a party at six in the evening had not caught on. To avoid the problem at his own party, Waugh invited his friends to tea at 4.30pm and started serving cocktails at 5.30pm.

The cocktail inspired a host of gadgetry and artefacts - cocktail shakers, glasses, swizzle sticks, cocktail mats and of course those marvellous Art Deco cocktail cabinets - the last word in kitsch.

Ernest Hemingway was a great Martini drinker and his characters are often found drinking them - see particularly "The Sun Also Rises" where there is a martini drinking session towards the end of the novel.

The Bright Young Things

The early part of the 20th century after the First World War was a time of enormous change and social upheaval. Nineteen million young men had died in pointless battles and, when the war ended, there was a desire to see the bringing down of the old order which had created such misery and destruction.

In Galsworthy's "The Forsyte Saga", Montague Dartie, although glamorous, is perceived as a bit of a cad as he is drinking a cocktail when Queen Victoria's funeral cortege passes his club.

The novels of Evelyn Waugh evoke the zeitgeist of the 1920s and '30s. The outrageous behaviour of his "Bright Young Things", their endless parties, the fast cars, the outlandish cocktails - all these point to an absolute determination to put the misery of the war behind them and to make up for lost time. Hence the almost hysterical gaiety, fuelled by desperation and cynicism.

In the frantic desire to forget death and celebrate life, the cocktail played an important role. The cocktail was new and everything new from Picasso to the automobile was embraced with enthusiasm. The cocktail celebrated the modern and the urbane. It was sophisticated and fun: to drink it was to identify with the young and the fashionable, an image that the cocktail has retained to this day.

In the 1930s Booth's published an Anthology of Cocktails where a number of personalities gave their favourite cocktail recipe and said what they thought of each drink.

Our choice for
IVOR NOVELLO

STAR COCKTAIL

⅓ BOOTH'S DRY GIN
⅓ CALVADOS — APPLE BRANDY
1 Dash French VERMOUTH
1 Dash Italian VERMOUTH
1 Teaspoonful GRAPE FRUIT JUICE

Shake and strain into cocktail glass.

Thought for the occasion:
"RAPTURE MAY BE CARELESS, BUT YOU CAN'T ATTAIN IT UNLESS YOU'RE CAREFUL TO ASK FOR BOOTH'S."

GIN PAHIT

*A standby of the British Raj
and rather like a Pink Gin.
Fill an old fashioned glass
to within ⅛" from the top
with gin.
Add 3 dashes Angostura
Add 2 dashes Absinthe
Several large cubes of ice
Stir. Add a twist of lemon to
each drink.*

GIN 'N' IT

*1 part Italian Vermouth
3 parts gin
Make the same way as gin
pahit*

GLOOM CHASER

*A basic dry martini with
2 dashes absinthe
2 dashes grenadine
Make the same way as a
dry martini*

Aromatic Cocktails

The definition of a cocktail is "an iced drink made of spirits, bitters, flavouring and sugar". In practice this tends to be a base, a modifier which is either bitters or another liquor, fruit, carbonated drinks and/or fruit juice.

Gin is the most commonly used base for cocktails because it does not need the addition of other drinks to make it palatable and its flavour is so subtle it will blend with all manner of flavours in a mixed drink. Of all the common liquors, gin also gives the quickest lift which is important because a cocktail should properly be drunk before a meal as an aperitif.

The aperitif cocktail should whet the appetite - not dull it - which pretty much rules out mixed drinks with unlikely names generally featuring exotic locations in the Caribbean and little paper parasols. Too often these concoctions contain

large quantities of sugar, cream, fruit or eggs and tend to induce nausea. They should be avoided.

Gin cocktails are divided into two distinct types - the aromatic and the sour. The aromatic type will use bitters or one of the various aromatic wines such as French or Italian vermouth. The Sour is so called not because it tastes sour but because it is modelled on the various Sour recipes i.e. it will contain lemon or lime juice, spirits and sugar or sweetening.

BRONX
1 part French vermouth
1 part Italian vermouth
1 part orange juice
6 parts yellow gin
Shake with cracked ice.
Drop a twist of orange peel
into each glass

GIMLET

3 parts dry gin

1 part Rose's Lime juice

Shake in a shaker with ice.

Pour.

SINGAPORE SLING

1 teaspoon Sugar Syrup

Juice of ¼ large lemon or

½ large lime

1 pony Cherry brandy

1½ jiggers Gin

1 dash Angostura

Shake and strain into 8 oz

highball glass. Fill glass with

soda water. Some recipes

call for the addition of a

pony of Benedictine. A slice

of lemon peel should be

twisted over and dropped

into the drink.

The Best Sours

In addition to the two basic types of cocktail, the aromatic and the sours, there are also distinct variations between true cocktails and other gin drinks. Gin and tonic for example is not a cocktail but a Tall Drink. Other tall drinks belong to the Collins family and probably the most well-known is the John Collins which is made as follows:

Squeeze the juice of a lemon into a tall glass.

Add 1 heaped teaspoonful of sugar, 2 oz of gin and plenty of ice.

Fill the glass with soda water.

GORDON'S
SPECIAL
OLD TOM

the
finest quality
sweetened gin
obtainable

FINEST CANE SUGAR USED

WHITE LADY
1 part Cointreau or
Triple Sec
2 parts lemon Juice
8 parts Gin
1 Egg White to each
2 drinks
Put all the ingredients
except the gin in a shaker
with cracked ice. Shake
vigorously until thoroughly
mixed. Add half the gin,
combine and shake. Then
add the rest and shake well.
Strain into chilled cocktail
glasses

The Tom Collins traditionally was always made from Old Tom Gin which is now unobtainable. They are both essentially Slings.

Then there are the short drinks. At the same time the Cocktail was being perfected, the favourite mixers for gin lower down the social scale were peppermint, orange squash and ginger beer. A popular mixed drink amongst working men was The Dogs Nose - a pint of beer with a glass of gin added.

Today the favourite mixers for gin are bitter lemon, orange, tonic water of course, and, in Spain, Coca-Cola.

DUTCH GIN

Geneva or Jenever remains the Dutch national drink and is widely drunk throughout Holland. The typical characteristics of modern geneva hardly differ from those of centuries ago although modern production methods have enabled a greater purity and consistency to be achieved. The most internationally well known brands of geneva are made by Bols and De Kuyper both of whom have been distilling in Schiedam since about 1695. In distilling history terms Schiedam is just as important as Cognac or the Scottish Highlands.

PART VI: GIN TODAY
The End of the Cocktail Age

The Cocktail Age effectively ended in the 1930s, dealt a fatal blow by the Depression. During the war gin was hard to get hold of because of shortages and the quota system. Good gin was particularly hard to track down because, as in the bad old days of prohibition, there was a thriving black market for adulterated gin and noxious, gin-like substances.

For some years after the War, gin was in short supply but by the early '50s with the end of Rationing, the situation had stabilised.

One thing was clear: London Dry gin was now indisputably the dominant gin type. Old Tom was still made, notably by Gordon's, and, for a long time, flavoured cordial gins like Orange Gin and Lemon Gin were also produced. The purity and sophistication of the London Dry gins however had set the standard for gin and created a market for the premium products.

Despite the growth in popularity of other white spirits vodka and white rum, gin has continued to hold its own, and is known and appreciated throughout the civilised world as much for its unique heritage and character as its quality and distinction. The great distilling firms still produce their gin according to traditional methods and maintain the tradition of the quality and exclusivity of this most subtle and pure spirit.

Geneva is a malt spirit distilled from the mash of barley, maize and rye and rectified with the juniper berries and other botanicals to create the characteristic taste which is stronger, more malty and more fiery than English gin. Geneva should always be served well chilled and drunk either neat or on the rocks since it is not a good mixer.

Yes, we must join the ladies!

say **BOOTH'S**
AND AVOID ARGUMENT!

The name quinine is derived from the Peruvian native word, "quina" or "kina" bark. Spaniards invading Peru found natives using the bark as a cure for fever, particularly malaria. In 1638 the wife of the Viceroy of Peru, Countess Cinchona was cured of fever by a local physician using the bark. She vowed to make her miracle cure widely known and it is said that it was she who brought back to Europe the bark powder which became known as cinchon in her honour. It was also called Peruvian or Jesuit's bark.

Tonic Water - From Medicine to Mixer

The principal ingredient of tonic water is quinine which imparts the characteristically bitter taste.

The origins of the drink are to be found in the days of the British Raj. In India and other parts of the fever-ridden Empire, European residents were prescribed a daily dose of quinine to combat malaria. The bitter flavour of the quinine was made palatable by adding sugar and diluting the resulting mixture with water. One can easily imagine a lonely colonial administrator, stranded in some far flung outpost, deciding to liven up his daily medicine with the addition of gin, little realising how momentous his decision would be.

Early in the 19th century, Indian Quinine or Indian Tonic Water, so-called because of its associations with India, became a standard beverage somewhat like a cordial or a modern 'health drink'. British colonials returning from India had brought the taste for this bitter tonic drink back home with them and there were soon manufacturers ready to supply the demand.

Commercial production of proprietary bottled tonic water began at a surprisingly early date. In 1858, one Erasmus Bond was granted a patent for "an improved aerated tonic liquid", and although Bond tried to keep his recipe a secret, there were soon many brands of tonic water on the market. The best known manufacturers are Schweppes who added Tonic Water to their range of bottled drinks in the 1870s.

Tonic water was very much a British taste until relatively recently and was almost unknown in North America until Schweppes started bottling there under franchise in 1953. It is now popular world-wide both as a mixer for spirits and on its own.

Jacob Schweppes was born in Germany in 1740. In the 1780s he perfected a technique of making mineral water and in 1798 set up a small factory in Drury Lane. The company prospered and, in 1851, was appointed the official provider of soft drinks to The Great Exhibition where 1,092,337 bottles of Schweppes' soda-water, lemonade and ginger-beer were sold.

Modern tonic water contains only minuscule amounts of quinine except in the tropics where the medicinal value of quinine tonic water is still recognised.

Cinchon had certainly reached Europe by the 18th century through Spain and Italy (where it is still a popular flavouring in many drinks). Seeds of the tree were stolen from Peru by the German Dr. Hasskari on behalf of the Dutch and the trees were then successfully cultivated in Indonesia and later in India.

DESIGNER GIN AND TONIC

The Perfect Gin and Tonic

In July 1995 Gordon's linked up with design guru Sir Terence Conran to produce a striking, limited edition Gordon's & Tonic in a can. It was the first time that Sir Terence had ever designed a drinks can.

Gin and tonic water are such well suited companions that one would almost think they were made for each other, the dryness of one blending perfectly with the bitterness of the other to create an invigorating and sophisticated, quintessential English drink.

The definitive gin and tonic should be cold, refreshing and bitter clean. To achieve this, follow a few basic rules:

* Always use a good quality London Dry gin like Gordon's, Beefeater or Bombay Sapphire. You could keep it in the freezer for extra coldness.

* Never accept tonic from a spray gun or use a bottle that has been standing opened. The first is over-sweetened, the second will have lost its fizz. Your tonic water should always be a freshly opened bottle of Schweppes or some other premium brand.

* Then take a tall glass with a heavy bottom which will make the bubbles in

the tonic last longer.
You'll notice a
difference if you
frost the glass in the
freezer beforehand.

The astonishing bubble photography which featured in Gordon's 1995 Innervigoration advertising campaign was created by working with up to 18 separate transparencies. Work on just a small part of the lemon took over 4 hours.

- Ice is crucial. Ideally
the ice will have been
made in one of the new
types of machine which freeze
very quickly and produce dry, hard, and 'clean' i.e.
transparent, ice. The wet variety melts too quickly,
turning the drink to slush and diluting much of its
flavour. The same is true of crushed ice. At home you
should use large chunks of ice and pat them dry with
a tea towel. (Peter Dorelli of The American Bar at The
Savoy, who makes a superb gin and tonic, advises that
proper ice is the most important ingredient of the gin
and tonic). Put plenty of ice in the glass and slowly
pour in a generous measure of gin.
- Add enough tonic to fill the glass.
- Finish with a hefty chunk of lemon or, for a slightly
different flavour, try a wedge of lime. Some gin experts
claim that lemon or lime spoil the flavour. Try it without
and see which you prefer.

Stir to release the juniper flavour, enjoy.

*INNERVIGORATION
CAMPAIGN*

*Gordon's 1995
'Innervigoration' campaign
successfully promoted the
concept of the perfect gin
and tonic.*

The most convincing explanation for the origins of the Martini is that it was first served in about 1912 in the fashionable Knickerbocker Hotel in New York and was the invention of the head barman, Signor Martini, hence its name. Martini's recipe called for half and half imported London Dry gin and French vermouth with a dash of orange bitters.

Debate rages on the subject of the perfect Martini particularly on the correct proportion of gin to vermouth. Suggestions vary from 3:1 gin to vermouth, to gin which has had vermouth sprayed on it from a perfume atomiser.

The Martini

Today there are about 7,000 officially recognised cocktails, many of which are gin based. The true connoisseur however will confine himself to a few, very good cocktails. Of all the aromatic cocktails, the most perfect, indeed one of the great gin drinks of all time, is unquestionably the Dry Martini.

The dry Martini is a drinker's drink: strong yet subtle, it

Dean Martin, a great Martini drinker, used to say it was enough to show the bottle of vermouth to the gin. Others claim that light shining through a bottle of vermouth on to the gin is perfectly adequate.

makes instant and powerful impact. It is a metropolitan drink, a sure fire remedy for the ills of urban warrior. Some have even claimed that it has been America's most important contribution to world culture.

A dry Martini is a dry Martini only when it is made with a premium London dry English gin and French, not Italian, vermouth. There has been much argument as to the correct way to make the perfect Martini. The definitive Martini is made as follows:

- Into a jug or large glass with large cubes of ice pour 1 part good quality French vermouth
- 7 parts premium brand London Dry gin

Stir, and pour over the ice into chilled cocktail glasses. Twist lemon peel over the top. Add an olive. If you add a small pickled cocktail onion, it becomes a Gibson. If you shake the Martini it becomes a Bradford despite what James Bond might have had to say on the subject.

There is an old chestnut about the traveller's essential rescue pack. It should contain gin, vermouth, ice, lemon, a shaker and a glass. When you are completely lost or in desperate straits, all you have to do is to unpack it and start making a Martini. It is guaranteed that an American will instantly pop up, no matter where you are, to tell you how to do it properly.

Sauce Escabèche

Olives cassées aux herbes

Olives aux Herbes de Provence

Farcies Poivrons

Vermouth is white wine, blended, fortified and made aromatic through the addition of herbs and spices, chiefly wormwood which is also the basis for absinthe.

Beefeater has always enjoyed great export success. The company was already exporting in 1900 with shipments of gin to Montreal. During the '50s, Eric Burrough built up export markets, particularly that of the United States. The coronation of Queen Elizabeth caused immense interest in the British and British products. James Burrough took advantage of this by emphasising the name 'Beefeater' on their imported bottles in the USA and began to hit USA domestic gin sales hard. In 1963 Burroughs was the biggest gin exporter in the British Isles. Today Beefeater exports 500,000 cases of gin a year to Spain where they drink it with coca cola.

PART VII: THE GREAT GINS
BEEFEATER - complex, rounded, citrus, clean

James Burrough founded the company which produces Beefeater gin in 1863 when he bought the firm of John Taylor & Son, rectifiers of gin and liqueurs. James Burrough had trained as a pharmacist and had travelled widely in the United States as a young man. On his return to London he quickly saw the commercial opportunities for making a superior quality gin. He perfected his own recipe and began making Beefeater Gin some time after 1863.

In 1897 James Burrough's sons took over the business. The company remained in family control until 1987 when it was acquired by Whitbread. It is now part of the Allied-Lyons Group. In 1908 Burroughs moved from Chelsea to Lambeth where it has remained - the only major distillery still based in London.

Beefeater Gin is still made to James Burrough's original recipe which is known to contain juniper, coriander, citrus peel and angelica - the other ingredients remain a closely guarded secret. Beefeater owes its distinctively fresh taste to the quality of its grain spirit which is 90% wheat and 10% malt and is made in Scotland at factories who principally make spirit for whisky distilling.

When the botanicals are added, the mix is steeped for 20 hours before re-distilling. The whole process is carefully supervised by Master Stillman, Desmond Payne, on whose judgement and skill alone the quality of Beefeater depends.

For the home market Beefeater retains its strength at 40% proof. Like many other brands Beefeater is sold at higher strengths for export including one at 57%.

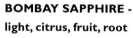

It takes between six and six and a half hours for the run of the distillation to be complete.

BOMBAY SAPPHIRE - light, citrus, fruit, root

Bombay Sapphire in its stylish translucent blue bottle has become enormously popular in recent years.

Its distinctive flavour is the result of using no less than ten botanicals in the mix. To the commonly used flavourings of juniper, coriander, angelica and lemon peel are added orris root, liquorice, cassia bark, almonds, cubeb berries from Java and the wonderfully named grains of paradise from West Africa.

Every distillation is different and can only be judged by the master distiller who 'noses' the spirit to decide when the botanicals have released the best of their flavour.

At the distillery in Cheshire, Bombay Sapphire is distilled by the now rare racking method. The pure grain spirit is heated from below to pass through the botanicals which are housed in a separate perforated copper basket above the still. The spirit is therefore in a vapour form when it meets the botanicals and slowly absorbs their flavours.

The result is a balanced spirit with a hint of spiciness, an exotic and subtle flavour which imparts a pleasant fragrance with a dry finish.

Booth's advertising was aimed at a sophisticated market and, for example, used colour before any of the other major brands.

BOOTH'S LONDON DRY GIN -
light, sweet, highly flavoured

It is thought that Booth's is the oldest gin-distilling firm still in existence. The first reference to the Booth family's involvement in the wine trade is to be found in a document of 1569 and it is likely that the Booths were producing gin in early 18th century London because most wine merchants did. The first official record of Booth's Distilleries dates back to the Directory of Merchants for 1778 which lists a Philip Booth & Company in Clerkenwell.

In the following century Sir Felix Booth expanded the business and turned it into the largest distilling company in England. Booth's was a family owned firm until 1896 when on the death of the last male Booth, it became a limited company.

During the 1920s and '30s Booth's was the premium English gin, expanding and diversifying in a very innovative way and selling particularly well in the export market. Booth's Dry gin was distinguished by its very slightly golden colour, the result of being aged in sherry casks.

Although it remains popular, Booth's Gin is a shadow of its former self. It is now made from a molasses base which gives it a much more highly flavoured and sweeter taste. It is sold widely in supermarkets throughout the UK and Continental Europe.

Unfortunately for Booth's its distinctive golden colour contributed to its later fall in popularity because Booth's marketing strategy was focused on purity and cleanness at the same time that the competing clear gins were communicating the same message far more effectively.

BURNETT'S WHITE SATIN -
aromatic, citrus, rounded

Sir Robert Burnett joined the company that bears his name in 1770. The original company is supposed to date back to 1679 so would have been in business at the time when commercial distilling started in England.

Sir Robert Burnett was clearly an entrepreneur of the first order. The quest to find a recipe to make a quality London gin was only the first step in a long and successful career. He became Sheriff of London in 1794 and was knighted the following year.

White Satin still bears the name of its founder in its branding and is produced to the original recipe. It is a quality London distilled gin which has retained a loyal customer base who prefer a traditional smoother, more aromatic taste.

Between 1924 and 1963 the company belonged to the Distillers Company and since 1963, it has been part of Seagram UK Ltd.

PLYMOUTH GIN -
light, root, earthy,

Plymouth Gin can only be so described if it is made in Plymouth.

The Coates family established a distillery in 1793 in the old Black Friars Monastery in Plymouth. It was here that the Pilgrim Fathers were supposed to have had their last meeting before they set out in the Mayflower for America in 1620.

Plymouth Gin is still made by Coates & Co. who are now, with James Burrough, part of the Allied-Lyons group. It owes its distinctively full flavour to its particular recipe and the purity and softness of the Dartmoor water used in its manufacture.

The gin made in Plymouth retained its more aromatic flavour after the introduction of the London Dry style. Plymouth Gin contains a higher than usual proportion of root ingredients hence its earthy, rooty, taste which differs markedly from the lighter fruitier taste of other gins. It has a strong local following and it is interesting to compare the difference between it and London Dry.

Because of its location, Plymouth Gin has always had strong naval associations, and is still preferred by the Royal Navy who claim a proper Pink Gin is only made with Plymouth gin.

SLOE GIN

For another different gin taste, try sloe gin which can easily be made at home. Half-fill a large clear bottle with sloes which should have been pricked, preferably with a silver needle. Add 2 inches of castor sugar. Top with good full-strength gin. Close bottle firmly. Over the next 3 months shake the bottle whenever you remember. Leave for as long as you can bear. Decant, straining carefully into clean bottles. Alternatively, take the easy option and buy a bottle of Gordon's Sloe Gin.

Gilbeys' advertising was always very successful and ahead of its time. The original company of 1857 had been launched by a national newspaper campaign which was so effective that, within months, the new company had over 20,000 customers.

GILBEY'S - smooth, citrus, dry

Walter and Alfred Gilbey were the sons of a Bishops Stortford coach operator. Returning to London in 1857 from active duty in the Crimean War, the two brothers set up a wine business in Soho importing fine wines from the Colonies to cater to the needs of a growing prosperous middle class. They soon expanded into smarter premises in Oxford Street.

In 1867 the Gilbeys moved into the famous Pantheon building further along Oxford Street and their business mushroomed when they started producing Gilbey's gin at their own distillery in Camden Town.

Success was rapid and by the 1920s Gilbey's had distilleries operating in Australia and Canada. Prohibition did no harm at all and the Pantheon offices were soon dispatching specially packaged consignments of gin for shipment to Antwerp and Hamburg. From there they were shipped to outside the 12 mile limit and then were run into the States in fast boats past infuriated coastguards. Needless to say these customers paid in cash.

Unfortunately for the company, so popular was Gilbey's that it was soon being widely counterfeited by unscrupulous moonshiners. To prevent this, Gilbey's introduced its distinctive frosted bottles which could not be copied. It was not until 1975 that the company reverted to the traditional clear glass bottle. By this time it had distilleries in New Zealand, Uruguay, Namibia, East Africa, Swaziland, Mauritius and Mozambique.

Gilbey's is made in the same way using the same ingredients as it has been for over 120 years and has lost nothing of its quality and subtlety.

Gin is the least likely drink to produce hangovers. Research has shown that the hangover is related to the quantity of congeners in alcohol, i.e. the elements that are formed during fermentation or primary distilling.

GORDON'S - spirity, sharp, citrus, fruit

Alexander Gordon was of Scottish descent, born in London in 1742. He founded his business in London in 1769 and was a pioneer in his determination to make gin of a superior quality to any available at the time. He soon realised that the only way to achieve this was to distil only from pure spirit with carefully selected botanicals.

In 1786 Alexander moved his business to Clerkenwell where it remained until very recently. He died in 1823 and was succeeded by both his son and his grandson.

Charles Gordon sold the rectifying business in 1877 to John Currie & Co. of Bromley, Kent who produced neutral malt spirit for several distillers. Tanqueray had already been set up with backing from Curries as a guaranteed outlet

Some congeners disappear during maturation or are eliminated by rectification. In measuring congeners red wine comes top with 400, gin is right at the bottom with 3.

for its spirit and, in 1898, Gordon's and Tanqueray were merged to form Tanqueray, Gordon & Co. The move was of equal benefit to both companies, establishing them as the single most powerful force in English distilling.

Gordon's today is the best selling gin in the world with annual sales of over 6.5 million cases. It is exported to more than 140 countries and its distinctive bottles are found behind the counter of every top international bar. Through a combination of quality and its classic taste which is both earthy and peppery, Gordon's gin continues to 'refresh the world'.

Tanqueray's American fans have included Frank Sinatra, Bob Hope and John F. Kennedy.

TANQUERAY –
light, citrus, lemon, very dry

Tanqueray has been described as 'the Rolls Royce of gins' because of its exceptional quality.

From the foundation of the company by Charles Tanqueray in 1830, there has been a strong tradition of craftsmanship attached to the production of Tanqueray. Only the finest ingredients are used - juniper of course, coriander, angelica root, lemon and orange peels but also the less commonly used cassia bark and liquorice which contribute to its much vaunted dryness. Charles Tanqueray located his distillery close to a source of pure spa water in Bloomsbury. Today, while London Dry gin does not by law have to be distilled in England, all Tanqueray gin is.

The fame of Tanqueray spread rapidly, first to the outposts of the British Empire and then all over the world. Tanqueray and Gordon's had amalgamated in 1898 and in 1922 were acquired by the Distillers Company. After the Second

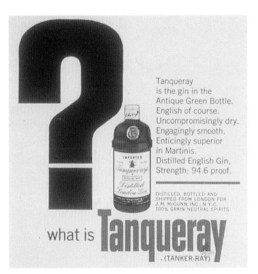

Tanqueray
is the gin in the
Antique Green Bottle.
English of course.
Uncompromisingly dry.
Engagingly smooth.
Enticingly superior
in Martinis.
Distilled English Gin,
Strength: 94.6 proof.

DISTILLED, BOTTLED AND
SHIPPED FROM LONDON FOR
J. M. McCUNN, INC., N.Y.C.
100% GRAIN NEUTRAL SPIRITS

what is Tanqueray
. (TANKER-RAY)

In 1995 rapper Snoop Doggy Dog released a very popular single and video "Gin 'n' Juice" which featured Tanqueray. Tanqueray is also celebrated in song by Rolling Stone Keith Richard.

Advertising for Tanqueray in the 'sixties' focused on a very effective "Pronounce it Tankeray" campaign.

World War a powerful marketing structure was created which allowed Tanqueray a premium export position as "Special Dry London distilled gin".

It is now the United States' best selling gin, accounting for over half the bottles sold. The Tanqueray bottle is the only one to be protected by world-wide patent. Contrary to the opinion of some experts, it was not modelled on the shape of 19th century fire hydrants but rather on the design of the cocktail shaker. The 'holdability' factor of the bottle plus Tanqueray's exceptional dryness which makes it the ideal gin for cocktails, explains why the gin has enjoyed such success internationally.

BIBLIOGRAPHY

Doxat, John 'The Gin Book'
Quiller Press 1989

Tony Lord 'The World Guide to Spirits'
Macdonald & Jane's London 1979

John Watney 'Mother's Ruin'
Peter Owen 1976

Lord Kinross 'The Kindred Spirit'
Newman Neame London 1959

Harrison Brian 'Drink and the Victorians'
Faber & Faber 1971

Sinclair Andrew 'Prohibition'
Faber & Faber 1962

INDEX